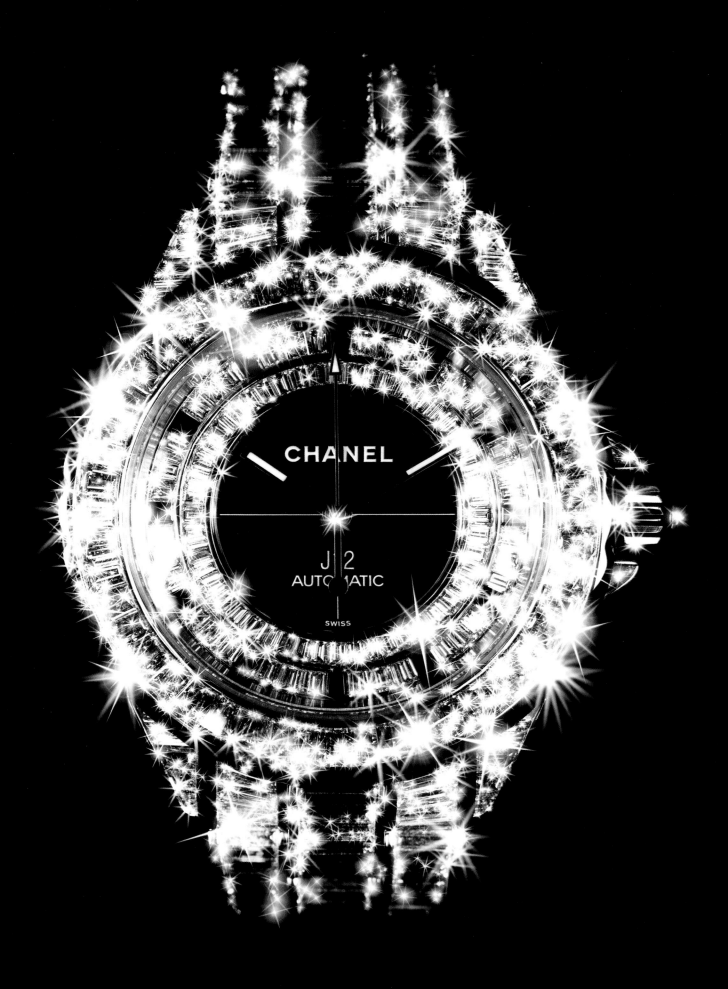

J 12

CHANEL

ETERNAL INSTANT

NICHOLAS FOULKES

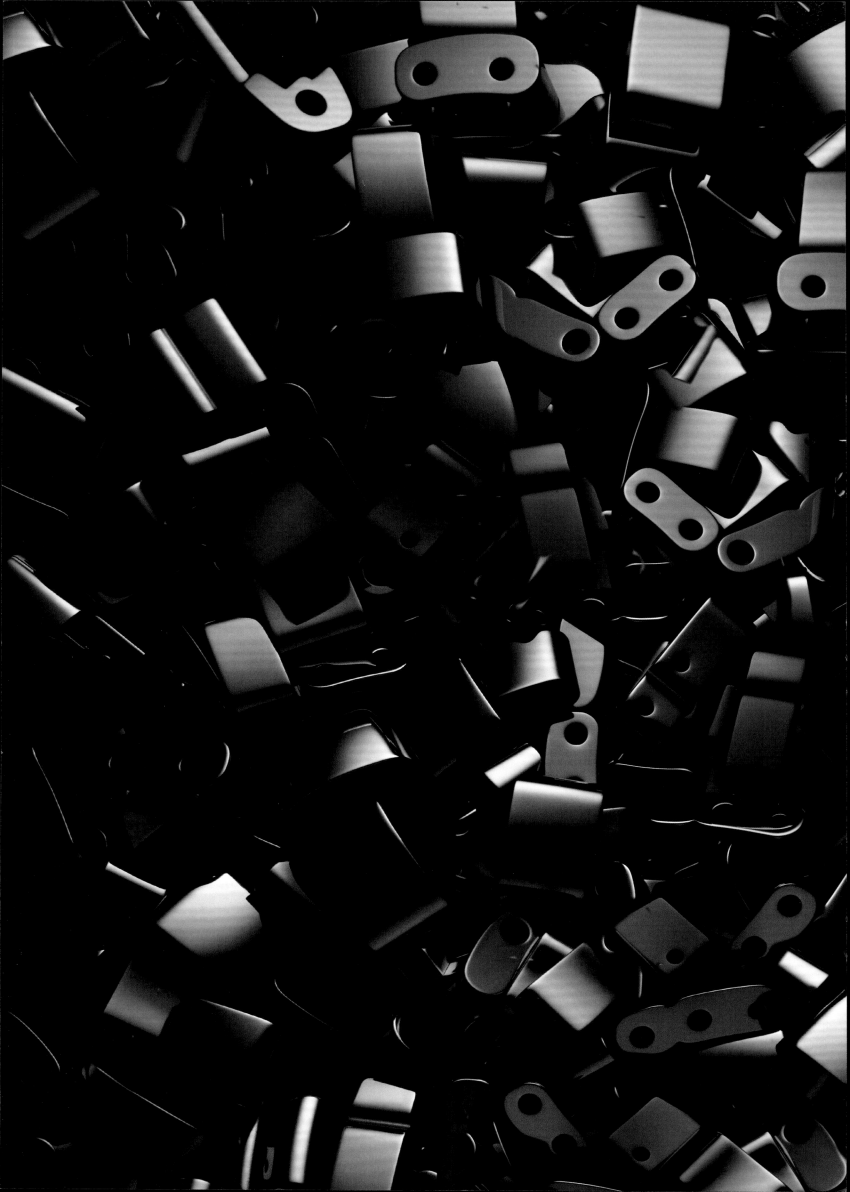

IF ONE WERE TO COMPRESS the J12 watch's two decades of innovation into an epigram, the sort of motto that old noble families engrave under their coats of arms, 'Technique at the service of design' is the maxim to which the J12 has been true.

Born with the century, the J12 has lived for twenty years. In those two tumultuous decades our world has changed more than anyone might have thought imaginable. Not so many new objects look as good today as they did in 2000.

With what seems almost comical hubris, towards the end of the twentieth century economist and political scientist Francis Fukuyama wrote his provocatively titled work *The End of History and the Last Man*, and posited that despite continuing events, mankind had reached the peak of its ideological evolution. He predicted the 'universalization of Western liberal democracy' and that any hiccoughs could be ascribed to flawed implementation of ideals. It was a very clever idea, brilliantly argued.

However, the first two decades of the current century have seen more 'history' than anyone could have predicted, more than anyone wanted and certainly more than anyone knew what to do with: economic, scientific, technological, political, theological, ideological, biological and, of course, medical.

At about the same time as campuses were debating whether history had ended, in Paris a distinguished-looking man, whose shock of white hair contrasted pleasingly with his black rollneck sweater, was sitting at a large slab-like desk in a prairie-sized office. The man was Jacques Helleu. His office was at Chanel, where he served as artistic director for Chanel fragrances, beauty products, watches and jewelry for almost half a century until his death in 2007. He was pondering the design of something that would never date.

The object that began to form in his mind was a wristwatch on an articulated bracelet, masculine and sporty, yet elegant, and the more he thought about it the more it became clear that this was a wristwatch that did not yet exist. The watch, executed in a glossy blackness of obsidian depth and adamantine hardness, would eventually become known as the J12. But the concept was ahead of its time, as Helleu later recalled: 'Originally in 1994 the technical means of producing the watch, as I wanted it, did not exist. No one was capable of giving me the shiny and resistant black that I needed.'[1]

Helleu was a remarkable man and by a fortunate accident of history he devoted his adult life to the house of Chanel. He had the mind of an engineer, the soul of an artist and the taste of a born aesthete: the J12 could only have happened at Chanel and only in Helleu's day. As well as requiring an as yet uninvented material possessed of an almost diamantine resistance, it needed a man of Helleu's strength of will, obduracy of character, eye for detail and uncompromisingly high standards to bring it into being.

Happily, Helleu belonged to the generation of mavericks who had shaped the modern luxury goods industry. He had also lived in the world of Chanel all his life. His grandfather Paul Helleu had painted the *beau monde* of Proustian Paris and it was in 1912 at the fashionable resort of Deauville that he had fallen under the spell of a young Gabrielle Chanel. Jacques's father Jean, both a painter of seascapes and a designer, worked as artistic director for Chanel. Perhaps unsurprisingly, N°5 was the first fragrance to fill the infant Jacques's nostrils, as it was the favoured scent of his mother.

Thus in 1956, Jacques continued the tradition established by his father and grandfather. 'I started out in the company at the age of eighteen at the request of Pierre Wertheimer, who asked me to take care of "the problems of taste."' Almost half a century later he was still asking himself 'what this enigmatic mission corresponded to.'[2] But whatever the mission, he accomplished it.

The son and grandson of artists who understood the house instinctively, Helleu worked with the greatest photographers and film directors – among them Richard Avedon, Irving Penn, Helmut Newton, David Bailey, Jean-Paul Goude, Ridley Scott and Baz Luhrmann – to create the image of the Chanel we know today. He was inspired by the work of great actors and directors to capture the essence of Chanel in the modern world. He worked with emblematic beauties: he cast the enigmatic Catherine Deneuve, acclaimed in 1968 as the most beautiful woman in the world, in Chanel advertising, and created some of his most memorable work with Carole Bouquet, Nicole Kidman and Vanessa Paradis. It is testimony to Helleu's far-sighted vision that many of the *égéries* he selected for Chanel returned to celebrate the launch of the new J12 in 2019: Ali MacGraw, Carole Bouquet, Claudia Schiffer, Vanessa Paradis, Anna Mouglalis and Keira Knightley.

By the early 1990s, when he sat down to imagine the watch that haunted his dreams, he was at the height of his powers, the eye of the fabled house. He had already developed one horological icon in 1987, the Première, a time-telling jewel, which took the Place Vendôme-inspired geometry of the stopper of the Chanel N°5 bottle and combined it with the interwoven leather and metal of the shoulder strap from the 2.55 handbag introduced in February 1955. Now, with the J12, Chanel was destined not just to repeat but to eclipse his first success as a watch designer.

The new watch was the distillation of decades of immersion in the world of Chanel. But so radical was the project that even a man as uncompromising as Helleu, who understood Chanel so acutely, was not going to find this easy.

'The most difficult part is always how to convince the others of the validity of an idea. Seven years have been necessary to achieve the J12 such as we know it,' he would say after the successful launch of the watch. As well as the absence of technology and material to make it, his task was even more difficult because 'no one saw the need for Chanel to meet a market for masculine watches.'[3]

The J12 became a receptacle into which he poured references from his world of uniquely elegant masculinity: the stark sculptural geometry of his Le Corbusier-designed house; the functional chic of the instrument panels of his 1958 Facel Vega HK 500 and his 1957 Bentley Continental; the drama and power of Raymond Loewy's monumental streamlined steam locomotives; the precision of the razor-like prow of a yacht slicing through the waves that would lend the watch not only its sharpness of line but also its name, after the J class racing yacht he so admired.

The J12 was to embody many firsts for Chanel: the house's first masculine watch, its first sports watch, its first automatic watch and its first all-black ceramic watch. Ceramic had been used in the watch industry before, but with the J12, this highly resistant material translated effortlessly to the world of fashion and luxury.

Although this was a watch Helleu wanted to wear himself, rather than simply a man's watch it was a *masculine* watch: a subtle but vital distinction. The J12 became an object like so many of Chanel's signature creations that had been conceived in the masculine world only to be subverted by Gabrielle Chanel. She had taken style influences from the male world and had made them her own. Chanel was the great liberator of women's bodies with clothes made from jersey, a fabric once used only for men's underwear. There were the jodhpurs she wore so she would not have to ride sidesaddle. She borrowed the Duke of Westminster's tweed coats and invented the tweed suit for women. She captured the olfactory memory of Grand Duke Dmitri Pavlovich's boots in a fragrance called Cuir de Russie – so named after the lingering aroma of the birch tar with which Russian soldiers dressed their footwear. She dared to do much that others would not; and so it was with colour. 'Before me, no one would have dared wear black,'[4] she would proudly boast.

In 2000 Chanel dared to launch a black watch. There had been black watches before, but here was a watch conceptualized around a nucleus of blackness, a watch for which black was not just a surface treatment but an inalienable part of its being. Then in 2003 technology advanced again and the J12, the quintessential black watch, became white – and in this starkest of contrasts it achieved immortality by expressing the fundamental axiom of Chanel: the dialogue between black and white. Ink on a page, spots on a die, night and day, the black bow and white shirt of evening dress, the lustre of a triple string of pearls heightened against black chiffon, a white silk shirt collar peeking over a black jacket: the exploitation and repetition of this, the simplest of contrasts, is achieved so effectively and burrows so deep into our visual understanding of the world; this primal contrast, the chiaroscuro effect of these two non-colours throwing each other into relief, is universally understood, and is utterly unarguable.

The stark, powerful, indisputable elegance of the juxtaposition of black and white defined the J12 and, standing on these unshakeable foundations, numerous variations appeared. But on the eve of its twentieth birthday, the J12 changed completely – and yet remained the same. Two decades of familiarity have bred only respect. It is with the deepest respect that Arnaud Chastaingt, director of the Chanel watchmaking creation studio, approached the redesign of the J12 in its twentieth year.

The most significant change has been mechanical. This new calibre 12.1, visible through the crystal caseback, is identified by the hoop-like profile of the tungsten rotor, so designed as to be able to accommodate gem-setting on high jewelry models. It is characteristic of the near-perfection of the watch that Helleu imagined over a quarter of a century ago that the most noticeable changes to the watch – the new movement, the specially shaped rotor, the ceramic case set with a sapphire glass that replaces the steel of the original – are invisible when the watch is on the wrist.

Other changes do not reveal themselves with just a glance. It is a relaunch of such forensic subtlety that rather like adapting to low light, which at first seems impenetrably dark, but from which, with time, shapes emerge to become recognizable objects, it takes time for the eye to adjust and become accustomed to spotting fine differences.

'First, I wanted to change everything,' admits Chastaingt. 'So the first two months I started working on this project I changed everything. Then I quickly understood that Jacques Helleu had already made the revolution when he launched the watch. So when I understood that, of course I had to keep the DNA of the original design. I knew then that this creative approach would be more the creative approach of the surgeon than a designer.' What followed was four years of forensic aesthetic surgery, during which, working at an almost cellular level, virtually everything about the J12 was changed... without a thing appearing to change.

Although 80 per cent of the components of this J12 are new, most of the changes are so microscopic as to be easily missed: a fraction of a millimetre here, a few microns there, a subtle change of font, the replacement of a flat surface with a barely perceptible curve... They are alterations on an almost philatelic level: tiny micro-adjustments. Maintaining the balance of proportions in order to make subtle changes while appearing to make none has, therefore, been crucial to a redesign so stealthy as to be all but invisible.

The calibrated rotating bezel now looks a little finer than it used to, because the number of notches has been increased from 30 to 40. While the notching has been increased by one third, the crown has been reduced in size by an equal proportion to sit more harmoniously between the two crown guards emerging from the case wall to embrace the winder.

The hour and minute hands are now the same width: filled with black Super-LumiNova pigment on the black J12 and in white on the white J12. But the sense of a photographic negative is introduced by the use of white hands for the black watch and vice versa. It is a visual witticism that would surely have amused Gabrielle Chanel.

Jacques Helleu would have enjoyed it too, while doubtless regretting that he could not achieve the perfect photographic negative with the hands himself. 'I think the white and black are the perfect negative,' explains Chastaingt delightedly. 'Jacques Helleu couldn't do the perfect negative with the hands. for the simple reason that at that time black Super-LumiNova didn't exist. Of course today we have the opportunity, and of course we use it on the new design.'

In essence, that is the nature of this redesign: bringing the J12 closer to the watch that Jacques Helleu wanted to make. One thing is for certain: this is not the 'End of History' for the J12, but the beginning of the next twenty years.

Nicholas Foulkes

"I wanted a watch for myself.
Virile, indestructible
and most of all black!
The first real black
luxury watch."

JACQUES HELLEU

J12

AUTOMATIC

7   5
6

SWISS ▫ MADE

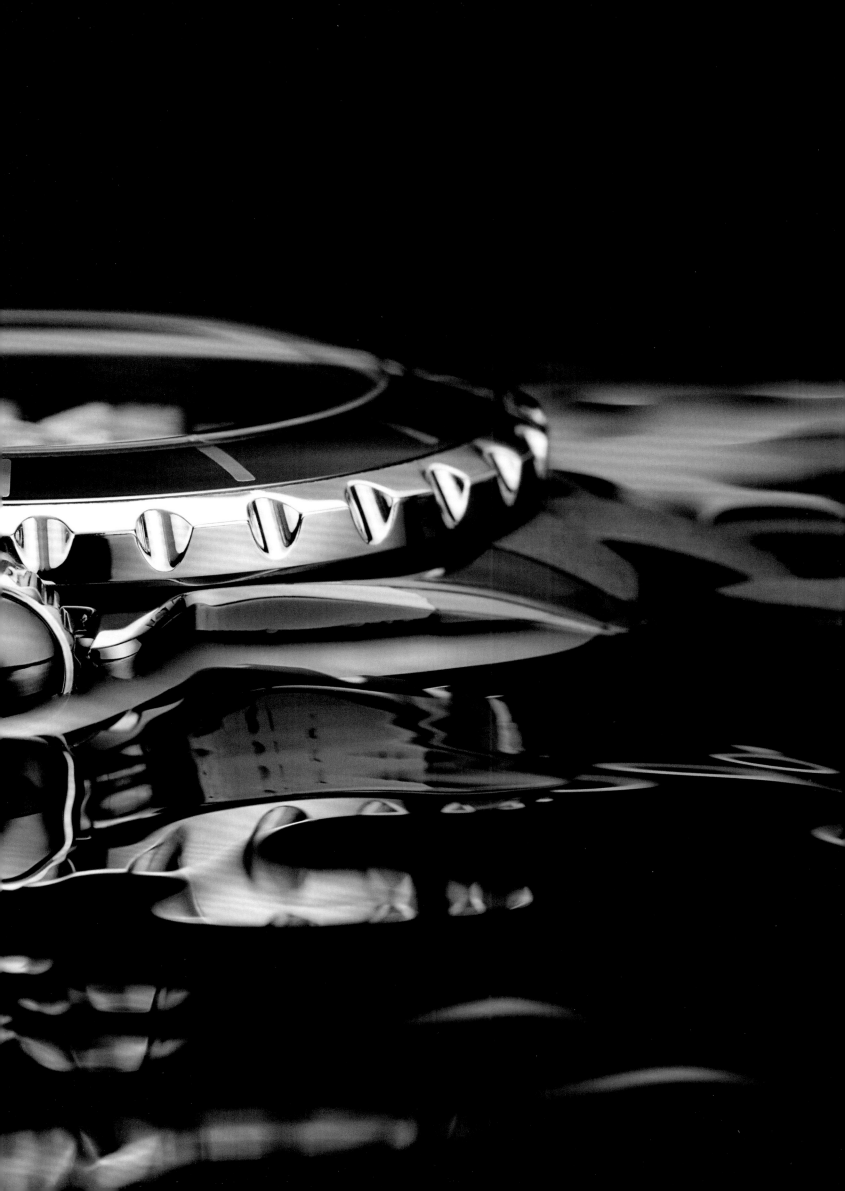

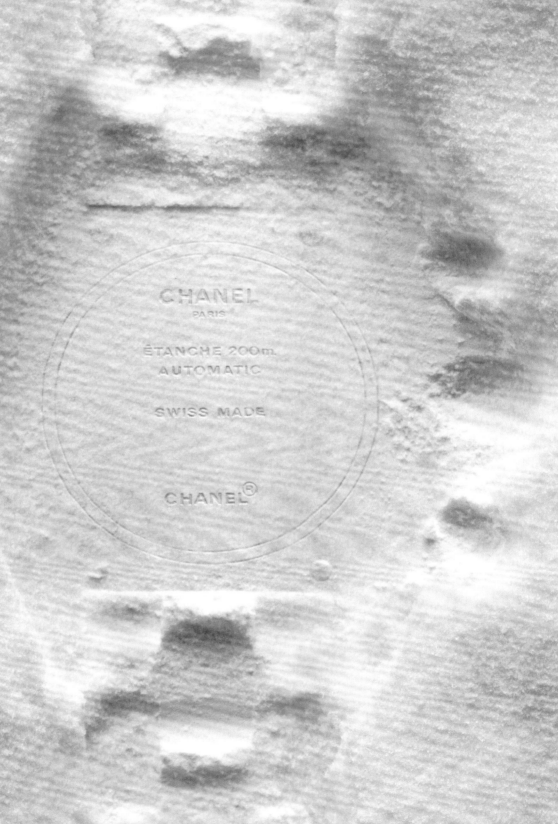

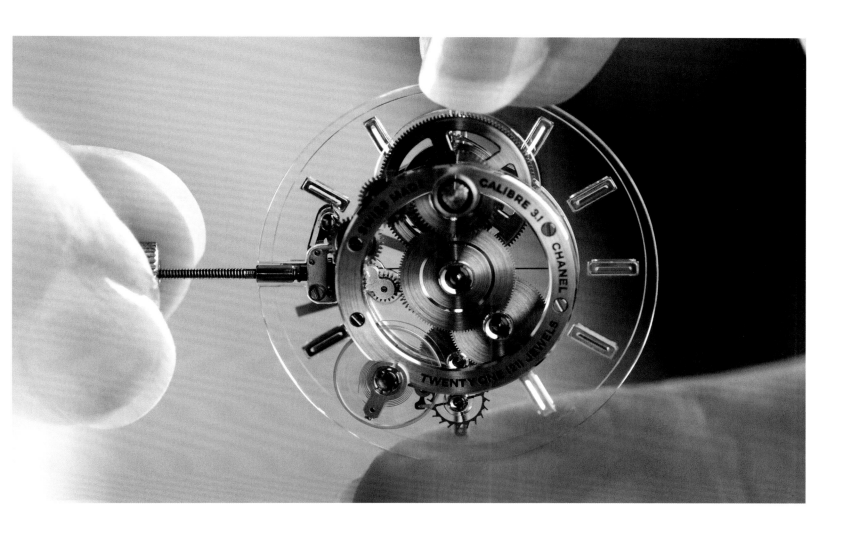

"You only make
a revolution once.
So I chose to change
everything
without changing
anything."

ARNAUD CHASTAINGT

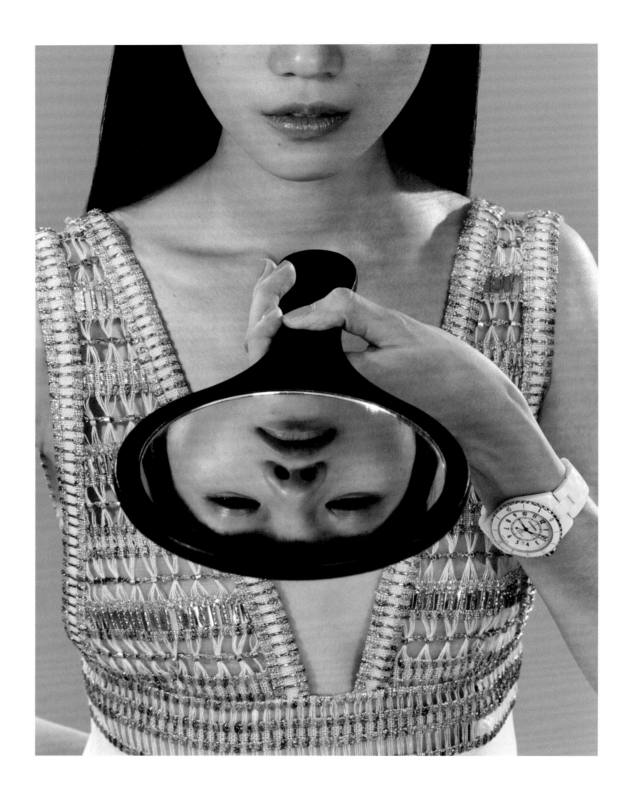

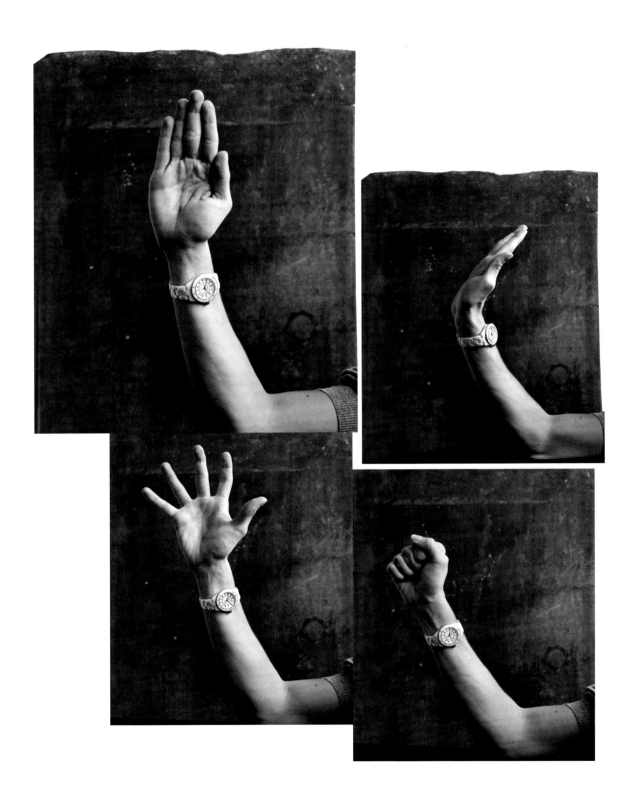

"I have said that
black has it all.
White also.
Their beauty is absolute.
It is the perfect harmony."

GABRIELLE CHANEL

PHOTO CREDITS

3
J12 watch in black highly resistant ceramic,
18-carat white gold and baguette-cut diamonds.
Numéro France, December 2007
© Photograph Guido Mocafico / 2007

4
Imprint of a J12 watch
© CHANEL / Photograph Kanji Ishii / 2002

6–7
J12 black highly resistant ceramic links
© CHANEL / Photograph Guido Mocafico / 2009

8
J12 watch sketch by Jacques Helleu
© CHANEL / Sketch by Jacques Helleu / 2000

14–15
Sail of a J class yacht
© CHANEL / Photograph George Harvey / Campaign J12, 2019

19
Jacques Helleu. Private collection

20
L'INSTANT CHANEL publicity campaign, featuring Monika Jagaciak
© CHANEL / Photograph Patrick Demarchelier /
L'INSTANT CHANEL campaign, 2015

21
ALLURE de CHANEL publicity campaign. Andrés Velencoso wears the
J12 Superleggera watch in sand-blasted black highly resistant ceramic
and aluminium, with black rubber strap
© CHANEL / Photograph Patrick Demarchelier /
ALLURE de CHANEL campaign, 2008

23
Gabrielle Chanel and the opera singer Marthe Davelli on a yacht, *c.* 1930
© CHANEL / Collection Denise Tual / 1930

24
Jake Davies wears the J12 Chronograph watch in black highly resistant
ceramic and steel. Claudia Schiffer and Jake Davies photographed
for the publicity campaign for the Spring-Summer 2008
Ready-to-Wear Collection
© CHANEL / Photograph Karl Lagerfeld / 2008

25
J12 Calibre 12.1 watch in black highly resistant ceramic and steel
© CHANEL / Photograph Guido Mocafico / 2019

26
ALLURE de CHANEL publicity campaign. Danny Fuller wears the
J12 Marine watch in sand-blasted black highly resistant ceramic
and steel, with black rubber strap
© CHANEL / Photograph Patrick Demarchelier /
ALLURE de CHANEL campaign, 2012

27
Hannah Ferguson wears the J12 Calibre 12.1 watch in white
highly resistant ceramic and steel. *Goop*, June 2019
© Photograph Jan Welters / Trunk Archive

28–29
J12 watch in black highly resistant ceramic and steel, 2000
© Photograph Kenji Toma / Trunk Archive

30–31
J12 watch in white highly resistant ceramic, steel and diamonds
© CHANEL / Photograph Kanji Ishii / 2003

32
Rico Broadwater, Rouzat, 1911
© Ministère de la Culture (France), MAP-AAJHL /
Photograph Jacques Henri Lartigue

33
J12 Marine watch in black highly resistant ceramic and steel,
with black rubber strap
© CHANEL / Photograph Guido Mocafico / 2010

34
J12-365 watch in white highly resistant ceramic and steel
© CHANEL / 2014

35
J12 watch in black highly resistant ceramic and steel
© CHANEL / Photograph Guido Mocafico / 2010

37
Camille Nevière wears the J12 watch in white highly resistant ceramic
and steel. *Gala* France, October 2011
© Photograph Bruno Poinsard / Trunk Archive

39
J12 watch in white highly resistant ceramic, steel and diamonds.
Elle White Dream Book, China, September 2012
© Photograph Sahteene & Stéphane Sednaoui

40–41
J12 watch in black highly resistant ceramic, steel and diamonds
© CHANEL / Photograph Kanji Ishii / 2002

43
From Lucien Clergue, *Langage des Sables*, 1980
© Photograph Lucien Clergue / Trunk Archive

44–45
Jacques Helleu with his J12 watch in black highly resistant ceramic and steel
at the wheel of a Facel Vega HK 500. *Stiletto* Hors Série, 5 May 2005
© Photograph Sonia Sieff

46
Bugatti Atlantic 57SC
© CHANEL / Groupe IMACOM / 2002

47
J12 Chronograph watch in black highly resistant ceramic and steel
© CHANEL / Photograph Kanji Ishii / 2002

48
J12 Superleggera watch in black highly resistant ceramic and aluminium,
2005
© Photograph Charles Helleu

49
Gaspard Ulliel wears the J12 Marine watch in sand-blasted black
highly resistant ceramic and steel, with black rubber strap.
L'Optimum, France, September 2010
© Photograph Paul Schmidt

50
J12 Superleggera watch in black highly resistant ceramic and aluminium
Jet Magazine, Hong Kong, September 2005
© Wah / *Jet Magazine*, Hong Kong

51
Kristen Stewart photographed for *Harper's Bazaar* UK, October 2019
© Photograph Alexi Lubomirski / Trunk Archive

52–53
Technical drawing of the J12 GMT watch
© CHANEL / 2007

54–55
J12 GMT watch in black highly resistant ceramic and steel
© CHANEL / 2007

56–57
J12 Calibre 12.1 watch in white highly resistant ceramic and steel
© CHANEL / 2019

58–59
J12 watch in white highly resistant ceramic and steel
© CHANEL / Photograph Guido Mocafico / 2009

60–61
CHANEL Manufacture. G&F Châtelain, La Chaux-de-Fonds, Switzerland
© CHANEL / 2009

63
Imprint of a J12 Chronograph watch
© CHANEL / Photograph Kanji Ishii / 2004

64–65
CHANEL Manufacture. G&F Châtelain, La Chaux-de-Fonds, Switzerland
© CHANEL / 2010

66–67
J12 Chronograph watch in white highly resistant ceramic and steel
© CHANEL / Photograph Kanji Ishii / 2004

68–69
J12 Chronograph watch in white highly resistant ceramic and steel
© CHANEL / Photograph Kanji Ishii / 2004

70–71
J12 Phantom watch in white highly resistant ceramic and steel
© CHANEL / 2013

73
Jacques Helleu wears J12 watch in black highly resistant ceramic and steel,
2000. In Jacques Helleu's hand, a Fulgurex 'Super Pacific Nord Carénée'
miniature locomotive. *Stiletto* Hors Série, 5 May 2005
© Photograph Sonia Sieff

74
Calibre 3.1 components, in-house skeleton movement designed and
assembled by the CHANEL Manufacture
© CHANEL / 2020

75
Calibre 3.1, in-house skeleton movement designed and assembled by the CHANEL
Manufacture with sapphire dial set with 12 baguette-cut diamond indicators
© CHANEL / 2020

76
Sketch of the Calibre 3.1, in-house skeleton movement designed and
assembled by the CHANEL Manufacture with sapphire dial set with
12 baguette-cut diamond indicators
© CHANEL / 2020

77
Calibre 3.1, in-house skeleton movement designed and assembled by the CHANEL
Manufacture with sapphire dial set with 12 baguette-cut diamond indicators
© CHANEL / 2020

80
J12 X-Ray watch in sapphire and 18-carat white gold, bezel set with
46 baguette-cut diamonds, fitted with Calibre 3.1, in-house skeleton
movement designed and assembled by the CHANEL Manufacture
© CHANEL / 2020

81
Arnaud Chastaingt, director of the CHANEL watchmaking creation studio
© Photograph Rasmus Mogensen 2020

82
J12 Chromatic watch in highly resistant titanium ceramic and steel.
San Francisco Magazine, USA, July 2011
© Photograph Peter Belanger

83
CHANEL Manufacture. G&F Châtelain, La Chaux-de-Fonds, Switzerland
© CHANEL / 2018

84
CHANEL Manufacture. G&F Châtelain, La Chaux-de-Fonds, Switzerland
© CHANEL / 2017

85
J12 Paradoxe watch in black highly resistant ceramic,
18-carat white gold and baguette-cut diamonds
© CHANEL / 2020

86–87
J12 watch in white highly resistant ceramic, white gold
and baguette-cut diamonds
© CHANEL / Photograph Guido Mocafico / 2010

88
J12 watch in white and black highly resistant ceramic, steel and diamonds
© CHANEL / Photograph Guido Mocafico / 2010

89
J12 Paradoxe watch in white and black highly resistant ceramic and steel
© CHANEL / 2020

90
Bella Nong wears the J12 Calibre 12.1 watch in white highly resistant
ceramic and steel. *Cittá Bella* Taiwan, July 2019
© Photograph Chou Mo

91
Adut Akech wears the J12 Calibre 12.1 watch in white highly resistant
ceramic and steel. *Chaos SixtyNine*, The Chanel Issue, July 2020
Courtesy *Chaos SixtyNine* magazine
© Photograph Luigi & Iango

92
J12 watch in white highly resistant ceramic, steel and diamonds.
Cosmopolitan, China, August 2016
© Photograph Xinlong Yu, East Image

93
J12 Calibre 12.1 watch in white highly resistant ceramic and steel.
Grazia, China, July 2019
© Photograph Li He

94–95
Saskia de Brauw wears the J12 watch in white highly resistant ceramic
and steel and an ensemble from the CHANEL Spring-Summer 2012
Ready-to-Wear collection
© CHANEL / Photograph Karl Lagerfeld / 2012

96
LE DUEL publicity campaign for the J12 watch. Grace Hartzel wears
the J12 watch in black highly resistant ceramic and steel
© CHANEL / Photograph Patrick Demarchelier / LE DUEL campaign, 2017

97
LE DUEL publicity campaign for the J12 watch. Grace Hartzel wears
the J12 watch in white highly resistant ceramic and steel
© CHANEL / Photograph Patrick Demarchelier / LE DUEL campaign, 2017

98
JD Samson wears the J12 watch in black highly resistant ceramic,
steel and diamonds. *Vogue Homme* France, Fall 2011
© Photograph Maciek Kobielski

99
ANIKV wears the J12 Calibre 12.1 watch in white highly resistant ceramic
and steel. *Glamour* Magazine, Russia, August 2019
© Photograph Erik Panov

100
J12 Calibre 12.1 watch in white highly resistant ceramic and steel.
M le Magazine du Monde, December 2019
© Photograph Joaquin Laguinge

101
Daan van der Deen wears the J12 GMT watch in black highly resistant
ceramic and steel. 'Watch Me Now', 2017. *Citizen K*, France, January 2018
© Photograph Justine Laeufer

103
J12·XS watch in white ceramic, leather, steel and diamonds
© CHANEL / Photograph Jean-Jacques Pallot / 2016

105
Jacques Helleu's hand wearing the J12 watch in black highly resistant
ceramic and steel. *Stiletto* Hors Série, 5 May 2005
© Photograph Sonia Sieff

106
J12 Tourbillon watch in black highly resistant ceramic, 18-carat white gold
and baguette-cut rubies. *Marie Claire*, China, June 2009
© Photograph Xinlong Yu

107
J12·XS watch ring in black highly resistant ceramic, 18-carat white gold
and diamonds
© CHANEL / Photograph Jean-Jacques Pallot / 2016

108
J12-G10 watch in white highly resistant ceramic, leather, steel and diamonds
© CHANEL / Photograph Jean-Jacques Pallot / 2014

110
J12 Calibre 12.1 watch in white highly resistant ceramic and steel.
L'Officiel Hommes Korea, November 2019
© Photograph Yongbin Choi

111
J12-G10 watch in black highly resistant ceramic, leather, steel
and baguette-cut diamonds
© CHANEL / Photograph Jean-Jacques Pallot / 2014

114
Nastya Abramova wears the J12·XS watch in white highly resistant ceramic,
leather, steel and diamonds. *Harper's Bazaar* China, October 2016
© Photograph Jin Jia Ji

115
Gabrielle Chanel, *c.* 1935. Photograph Man Ray
© Man Ray Trust/ADAGP, Paris and DACS, London 2020

116
Michelle McCallum wears the J12 watch in black highly resistant ceramic,
18-carat gold and baguette-cut diamonds. *Vogue* Germany, November 2009
© Photograph Valentin Jeck

117
J12 Phantom watch in black highly resistant ceramic and steel. *Numéro*,
France, November 2019
© Photograph Guido Mocafico

118–19
J12 Calibre 12.1 watch in black highly resistant ceramic and steel
© CHANEL / 2019

120
J12 watches in black and white highly resistant ceramic, steel and diamonds
© CHANEL / Photograph Zoé Ghertner / 2018

121
So Yu wears the J12 Calibre 12.1 watch in black highly resistant ceramic
and steel. *W* Korea, March 2020
© Photograph Kim Sinae

122
J12 Chromatic watch in highly resistant titanium ceramic and steel,
J12-G10 watch in black highly resistant ceramic, leather and steel.
Gala France, April 2017
© Photograph Bruno Poinsard / Trunk Archive

123
J12 Calibre 12.1 watches in black and white highly resistant ceramic
and steel. *Cittá Bella* Taiwan, July 2019
© Photograph Chou Mo

124
Cristiano Palmerini wears the J12 Calibre 12.1 watch in black
highly resistant ceramic and steel
© CHANEL / Photograph Thurstan Redding / OVER THE MOON campaign,
2019

125
J12 Calibre 12.1 watch in white highly resistant ceramic and steel.
The Nikkei Magazine Style Ai, Japan, May 2019
© *The Nikkei Magazine Style Ai* /Kodansha Co., Ltd.
Photograph Akinori Ito (aosora)

127
J12 Calibre 12.1 watches in black and white highly resistant ceramic,
steel and diamonds. *Harper's Bazaar* Middle East, May 2019
© Photograph Efraim Evidor / ITP

129
J12 watch in black highly resistant ceramic and steel.
Arena UK, December 2008
© Photograph Metz + Racine

131
Wataru Bob Shimosato wears the J12 Calibre 12.1 watch in black
highly resistant ceramic and steel. *Pop* UK, March 2020
© Photograph Charlotte Wales / Trunk Archive

132–33
Vanessa Paradis wears the J12 Calibre 12.1 watch in white
highly resistant ceramic and steel. *L'Uomo Vogue*, May 2019
© Photograph Peter Lindbergh. Courtesy Peter Lindbergh, Paris

134–35
Ali MacGraw wears the J12 Calibre 12.1 watch in black highly
resistant ceramic and steel. *Violet* UK, November 2019
© Photograph Pamela Hanson / Trunk Archive

136–37
Claudia Schiffer wears the J12 Calibre 12.1 watch in black highly
resistant ceramic and steel. *Vogue* Russia, January 2020
© Photograph Cuneyt Akeroglu

138
Gabrielle Chanel on the staircase at 31 rue Cambon, Paris, 1962
© Douglas Kirkland / Sygma / Corbis via Getty Images

139
J12 Mademoiselle watch in white highly resistant ceramic and steel
© CHANEL / 2017

141
Arizona Muse wears the J12 watch in white highly resistant ceramic
and steel and an ensemble from the CHANEL Spring-Summer 2017
Ready-to-Wear Collection
© CHANEL / Photograph by Karl Lagerfeld / 2017

142–43
J12 Untitled watches, case of 12 unique pieces in white highly resistant
ceramic and 18-carat white gold
© CHANEL / 2018

144
J12·20 watch motifs
© CHANEL / 2020

145
J12·20 watch in white highly resistant ceramic, steel and diamonds
© CHANEL / 2020

148–49
J12 watch in white highly resistant ceramic, steel and diamonds
© CHANEL / Photograph Kanji Ishii / 2012

The jewels on pages 37, 106 and 116 were made from designs
by Lorenz Bäumer.

ACKNOWLEDGMENTS

NOTES ON THE TEXT

1   Gregory Pons, *Temps Chanel*, Assouline, 2007, p. 15
2   Gregory Pons, *Temps Chanel*, Assouline, 2007, p. 15
3   Gregory Pons, *Temps Chanel*, Assouline, 2007, p. 15
4   Marcel Haedrich, *Coco Chanel*, Belfond, 1987

SOURCES OF QUOTATIONS

p. 17
Interview with Jacques Helleu, *L'Optimum*, June/July 2002
Interview with Jacques Helleu, *Montres Magazines*, Spring 2003

p. 79
Interview with Arnaud Chastaingt, May 2019

p. 113
Quoted in Jean Leymarie, *Eternal Chanel*, Thames & Hudson,
London, 2010, p. 122

The publishers would like to extend particular thanks to Hortense Izac, Alexandra Barcia, Cécile Goddet-Dirles, Odile Prémel and all those at Chanel who helped to make this publication possible.

Thanks are due to all the photographers, models and others who have kindly agreed to participate in this publication.

Photographers:
Cuneyt Akeroglu
Peter Belanger
Yongbin Choi
Lucien Clergue
Patrick Demarchelier
Efraim Evidor
Zoé Ghertner
Pamela Hanson
George Harvey
Li He
Charles Helleu
Kanji Ishii
Akinori Ito (aosora)
Valentin Jeck
Jin Jia Ji
Douglas Kirkland
Maciek Kobielski
Justine Laeufer
Karl Lagerfeld
Joaquin Laguinge
Jacques Henri Lartigue
Peter Lindbergh
Alexi Lubomirski
Luigi & Iango
Metz + Racine
Chou Mo
Guido Mocafico
Rasmus Mogensen
Jean-Jacques Pallot
Erik Panov
Bruno Poinsard
Man Ray
Thurstan Redding
Paul Schmidt

Sahteene & Stéphane Sednaoui
Sonia Sieff
Kim Sinae
Kenji Toma
Denise Tual
Wah
Charlotte Wales
Jan Welters
Xinleng Yu

Models:
Nastya Abramova
Adut Akech
ANIKV
Sask a de Brauw
Jake Davies
Daan van der Deen
Hannah Ferguson
Danny Fuller
Grace Hartzel
Monika Jagaciak
Ali MacGraw
Michelle McCallum
Arizona Muse
Camille Nevière
Bella Nong
Cristiano Palmerini
Vanessa Paradis
JD Samson
Claudia Schiffer
Watcru Bob Shimosato
Kristen Stewart
Andrés Velencoso
So Yu

First published in the United Kingcom in 2021 by
Thames & Hudson Ltd, 181A High Holborn, London WC1V 7QX

First published in the United States of America in 2021 by
Thames & Hudson Inc., 500 Fifth Avenue, New York, New York 10110

Chanel Eternal Instant © 2021 Thames & Hudson Ltd, London

Text by Nicholas Foulkes

British Library Cataloguing-in-Publication Data
A catalogue record for this book is available from the British Library

Library of Congress Control Number 2020940127

ISBN 978-0-500-02394-5

Printed and bound in Italy by Printer Trento